The Mermaid Sisters

Corinne Campo

DEDICATION

To my three beautiful daughters, Cameryn Rae, Quincey Grace, and Harley Rose you are so loved. You are all my forever treasures! I will always look forward to making beach memories on our annual summer vacation to Montauk, NY.

ABOUT THE AUTHOR

Corinne Campo grew up on the beaches of Long Island, NY. She currently resides in upstate New York with her husband Bryan and her 3 daughters. She enjoys cooking, exercising, concerts, skiing with her girls, and going on family trips to the beach.

It was that time of year again - sunny days, sandy toes, and salty air.

The sisters were headed to their favorite summer vacation spot, the beach.

The girls were excited for a week of fun! Building sandcastles, finding seashells, and swimming.

"What should we do first"? they all said. "Beach, pool? Who wants to play mermaids?" the oldest shouted.

Dressed up in colorful bathing suits and mermaid tails they frolicked along the beach and had the time of their lives.

The sisters loved to play make believe. They pretended to be mermaids swimming in the waters of Montauk, NY, looking for treasure at the bottom of the ocean.

They were excited to find shells, beachglass, old
jewelry and unique objects on the beach.

"When will we find the big treasure?"
the youngest sister asked.

"It's right here in front of us! Sisters are forever and the best treasure of all," the middle sister replied.

They all smiled and giggled. They realized she
was right. Sisters are treasures and they were
lucky to have each other.

"What's the best way to end our day at the beach"? said the oldest.

All three girls shouted, "Ice cream, Ice cream!"

ICE CREAM

The beach day was coming to an end. They took their mermaid tails off, wiped down their sandy sunkissed skin, and strolled into town.

Walking side by side, the sisters licked their ice cream cones and watched the sunset over the ocean.

"I can't wait to do this all again tomorrow," the youngest said. They all agreed.